PROPERTY OF THE
WINDSOR OF SAVOY

THE BLEEDING HEART CAFE

Poetry: A gritty look at how girlfriends talk, supporting each other through life.

By B. Gayle Dailey

"The Bleeding-Heart Cafe" cover is original art by the author.
This book and its contents are the property of the author.
All rights reserved. © June 1, 2015

INTRODUCTION

Bleeding, Not Broken

We've seen it all, my girly girls
Days filled with glories and with strife.
A swinging door of ups and downs
We've born some wounds and joys through life.

So yes, you'll see our bleeding hearts
But by the time our sorrow's spoken
Our girlfriends come to prop us up
And we're not even close to broken.

Girlfriends!

Across the valley
Across the hill
I feel your presence
And my heart rejoices
Girlfriends!
Love surrounds us.
Life may proceed!

Love and marriage are wonderful things, but there are some things a girl just has to talk over with other women. Entering new roles in life, most of us feel like girls again, so we also listen to older women, who we have learned, do know a thing or two. We don't stop there, for the generations behind us also have wisdom to share. But most of all, the women we call "Bosom Buddies" prop us up though the joyful and sorrowful times. The book cover was born from a sketch of bleeding heart blossoms, bosom buddies.

I love Helen Steiner Rice, but I'm not Helen. My life experiences have been dramatic and I have learned to savor the moments of peace, joy, love that hide between dramatic scenes. Some of these poems are gritty and some are lofty; some are from stories other people shared with me; some I just made up out of a thought, a word, a phrase I wanted to use. Any similarity to real people may just be your imagination!

Not Everything I Write Is About Us

I pillage countryside, my dears
for clever thought and phrase
Construct my prose and poetry
and watch your eyebrows raise.

You take it all to heart, my dears
quite sure you can see through
disguise and clever subterfuge
and think I speak of you.

You think I tell the tale of me
feel sympathy or guilt
when neither you nor I, my dears
appears in all I've built.

Not everything I write is about us!
Sometimes, I just make it all up as I go!

GIRLS ARE GROWN INTO WOMEN
BY WOMEN

Oh yes, girls learn to talk about life with each other by hearing their mothers and aunties discuss their own lives or making comments they think are unheard. Often, this must be accomplished by eavesdropping, for women do try to protect their young from becoming disillusioned. We've all heard them shush each other, mentioning "little ears." And then one day, well into puberty usually, they no longer change the conversation when you walk into the room. Then, your real education begins.

It never stops, for as friendships and trust levels deepen, women share intimate details about their bodies, their birthing experiences, their sexual encounters. But there are even more levels, dipping into raw emotions, sharing impressions of others; of how they think they may have been wronged and how they got revenge or learned to forgive. They will share their secret sorrows, jealousies, anger, their painful spiritual trials, doubting their faith and then their victories. It's a rich university of life in the kitchens and laundry rooms of the world!

Girls to Women

Here's one way we learned
What is lying ahead
When we'd face life full on
As grown women instead.

But as innocent girls
We hadn't yet learned
Eavesdropping is tricky
Details may get churned.

We hid in the background
And learned many things
Of secret affairs
Born of casual flings

Of rendezvous secrets
Divorces arising
Of lovers transformed
Into "Parties" despising.

(It wasn't intended
I'm sure, on their part
We fear lovers arriving
Who'll as bastards depart.)

The maladies whispered,
Embarrassing things
Of feminine woes
Such as Maxis with wings.

Of babies conceived
And of babies arriving

The pain and the joy
At their coming, their thriving.

Hot flashes, tight money
The loved ones at war
Sons "fooling with" girls
Others "fooled with" before.

The sorrows, deep hidden
That cut like a knife
Set aside, not forgotten
In the toils of life.

The horror of seeing
The ravage of time
On the flesh of those women
Shedding clothes in hot clime.

"Not us!" we declared
But then, we didn't know
In the raising of family
Self-absorption must go.

There's a toll that is laid
For such knowledge purloined
Goodbye Tooth Fairy, Santa
The real world's been joined.

Now we see what we missed
While enthralled by their news
Sacrifices they made
Growing us to their shoes.

The Porch

A pleasant rainy day,
mother, gramma and me,
recalling days gone by,
a bushel for us three.

There sitting in the swing,
newspaper on our knees,
together, safe and dry,
we'd talk and shell the peas.

It's how us younger ones,
were trained in family trees,
no sweeter teachers than
my mom, gramma, aunties.

I listened carefully,
and learned the rules of life.
I swelled with pride at last,
when trusted with a knife.

There, women's work was knit,
with precious memories,
no finer classroom than
the porch, the swing, just these.

Honest, the whiskey part in the next poem is complete fiction. In my growing-up circle of family and friends alcohol was only acceptable as part of a medicinal concoction. Good girls just didn't imbibe. But there were other circles that did, I learned much later.

That's Not Honey

We watched my elders rock and sip
When sorrows brought them by
Us cousins knew the day was sad
"Go play now, honey," mothers sigh.

So we would climb a tree or two,
Throw pebbles in the creek
And every now and then go check
Our grown-ups on the sneak.

The teapot on the banister
Our mothers on the swing
They balance tiny, dainty cups
Who would suspect a thing?

Invited to stay on the porch
As wives and mothers we
Learned that's not honey in the jar
There's whiskey in the tea.

For now we know, life lifts us up
Then dumps us with a flourish
And even Godly women need
Some tea that's braced with courage.

Angst

Angst, what a wonderful word
so dramatic
conveying scenes of apprehension
that even a young girl
could envision.

Angst, the poets love it, one word
that paints a thousand pictures
(I'd fling my hair and sigh,
clutching at my heart)
Angst tinged with hope
for better things to come.

Those days of girlhood dreaming
were the better things.
(Now I bow my head and softly
weep)
Ah, for those innocent days
filled with angst!
Before I came to know his older
brother,
Anguish.

Anguish

I watch your car pull away
and see sunshine glint
off the diamond ring
you just put on the finger
of my conniving sister.

Bills pile up under the mail slot.

"It's cancer,"
the Pediatrician said.

No milk in the house
the baby wails.

My child screams,
"I hate you!
You are a horrible mother!"

They were on that lost flight,
no word.

I stand alone by the grave
empty; numb.
waiting for the trifold flag
to be placed in my arms.

Agony

Oh, my child, my child
The pain I feel
I can't express.
I'm eating myself up
Giving and giving of myself
to you
Knowing it won't help
In the end.

With Words

With words I can paint pictures
Or write a memory book
With words I can uplift you
Or maim you with a hook.

With words I can deceive you
Inspire you with great truth
With words I can sow anger
With words can anger soothe.

With words at my discretion
A dove or hawk can be
With words I can be counted
Or cover tracks and flee.

With words firm in my conscience
Lay out a path I choose
With words I plot my life course
To grow or else to lose.

With words I build a circle
Of friends and family
But actions bring my words to life
For all the world to see.

There's At Least 100 Ways To Do It!

So it's "My way or the hi-way"?
Kiss my foot and call me gone!
At least a hundred ways to do it
But you're sure there's only one.

Life is filled with trails diverse
And every road leads right to Rome
But you only know your own way
Like a plug horse headed home.

Time to wake up and look outward
Please don't let life pass you by
Try a brand new way to do things
Lest your gray cells curl and die.

The Green Eyed Sisters

It did not begin in Eden
In the garden, no my friend
for the likes of Envy, green eyes
No beginning and no end

Envy's just the little sister
Nit who grows to be a louse
Often she's the subtle charmer
Who brings down your mighty house.

And there's Nosiness and Gossip
Cousins who drop by for tea
To partake a feast of goodies
Served by Curiosity.

Jealousy, who is the eldest
With her eyes of flashing green
Most vindictive and destructive
When she operates your spleen.

Best to tend to your own knitting
Nor for other's blessings lust
And you'll find your life most pleasant
Filled with folks that you can trust.

Time Walks a Line

If we had the eyes to see it,
Look somehow along the track
We'd see that time walks in a line
Forward, straight ahead from back.

What happened back, is up ahead
Costumed there in grown up gown
When we plant evil in the back
It waits ahead with vengeful frown.

The knives we throw, when we are back
When forward, earns us back a sword.
If while we're back, we do but good
Then forward, good be our reward.

Time walks a line we can't escape
No matter how we try it.
That seed we plant when we are back
Becomes our forward diet.

Dog In the Manger

Jealous!
Dog in the manger
green with envy
You don't want it
but don't want me
or anyone else
to have it

Hoarder!
Guarding your nest
of scorpion egg suspicions
like buried lights of hope
hidden under a bushel
Why, you'd sooner
let the world languish
in darkness
than share any
of your illumination.

Miser!
Rather than spend a penny
on anyone but yourself
you'd go hungry too.

My mamma told me
about her childhood,
of an old neighbor man
and the meal time Grace he said
"God Bless me and my wife,
my son John, and his wife.
Us four and no more!"

Aren't you a sight!
Poverty of the soul!
You have nothing
but buried treasures
eaten by the worms of time

Expiration Date

I once offered you my friendship
But you chose another way
And I had to go some distance
To avoid your quarrelsome fray.

Through the years
you've come to see me
In a different sort of light
You feel bad
about your meddling,
Building troubles for my plight.

Now you want to clear
your conscience,
Saw the clay
with which you're shod
And request of me forgiveness
As you're making peace with God.

Rest assured,
you're long forgiven
You were weak and I observed
Your self-worth
required proclaiming
Others worth as undeserved

I moved on
beyond your reach then
Making friendships firm and true.
Glad to hear
you're making progress
Wishing all the best for you.

Now please
don't misunderstand me
I don't plan to do re-play
We both move in different circles
And it's going to stay that way.

Opportunities, like coupons
Have an expiration date.
How we handle them's important
And may redirect our fate.

We may jump in to redeem them
'Ere a single brain cell's fired
Or ignore as unessential
Till we find they have expired.

Don't You See?

That if I plot and then succeed to change you
I've killed reflections of myself I need to know.
If I succeed in stifling your uniqueness
It's me who's stunted, me who cannot grow!

But still a lesson for us both is hidden
on this converging path He brought to be
And we both share His lesson, if we'll listen
Don't you see that I am you and you are me?

That blot or blemish found to be annoying
We think we see some evil in an eye
It's like we've looked into our own self-mirror
It's our own blemish that we loud decry!

God grant we welcome both the wit and wisdom
To drop our bristling stance and seek what's true
To turn from fantasy, and in pure courage
Proclaim the truth, that you are me and I am you!

Some Things Ain't Medicatible

Thank God for pharmaceuticals
Developed for our use.
Don't have to tolerate the itch
Or germs that turn bowels loose.

We've shots and pills for aches and pains
The flu and states of mind.
But there are things that ail some folks
A drug can't cure or bind.

No easy way of fixing up
A spirit that's gone sour
A temperament that's hateful
And plots mischief by the hour.

It takes a touch from God's own hand
As only God is able
Infusions of His healing love...
Some things ain't medicatible!

Sipping Life

Some people sip most daintily
of life, while others quaff!
And others still, seal up the cork
and never take it off.

So sip, or gulp, or even chug
but don't retreat in haste
Some vintages may leave you flat
until the after-taste.

Until I started writing poetry, I was ashamed of my dramatic flair. One day a young co-worker came and told me how much the next poem had helped her in dealing with an important relationship. That was the day I knew that this gift from God is not just for my own learning and growing process, or even my amusement, but for sharing with others.

We Won't Be Doing That!

I've collected some phrases
That can help, if you choose
To give up your role as door mat.
To stop folks from pushing
Where you don't want to go
Simply say
"We won't be doing that."

When the snoopers come calling
To price what you've bought
Ask your pay, what you eat,
where you go,
Slightly lift up your brow
Tilt your head and then ask,
"Why is it you're wanting
to know?"

"I can't speak for others
You must ask them yourself
I simply won't talk
at their backs."
"The decision's been made
It's not up for debate"
Stops controllers dead
right in their tracks.

"I'll forgive you for asking
Please forgive my non-answer
It's a personal matter you see."
"Yes I certainly know
Many things I won't tell
Confidences are secret with me!"

"I have dealt with this issue
It will stay in the past,"
Stops the stirrers
from stirring the pot.
When you speak just
these phrases
And add nothing more
You'll discover what power
you've got.

"That will not be possible"
(Don't ever add 'sorry!')
Holds manipulators at bay
Getting up off the floor
Is so simple my dears
Change your life with the words
that you say!

Stand up for yourself
But it needn't mean war
Be as firm but as kind as you can
Treat yourself with respect
By refusing control
If you lapse,
simply restart your plan

Just a word of advice
Please practice this first
Gently smile,
let your spirit be sweet.
The folks you're now facing
Never saw you stand up
And they might like
the new you they meet

I must credit Ann Landers
And Dear Abby Van B.
Who've assisted my stance
to "upright"
Many tips are from aunties
And strong women I've known
And some from my dreams
in the night.

There you go, hope it helps!
Take up courage and try
The first time is hardest, you bet!
But from there it gets easy
Just like running downhill
No more footprints will land
where you set.

I want to talk about what inspires my poetry. There is usually something I hear, see or feel that stimulates emotions, feelings, thinkings. I make a note, and sometimes it's years before I get back to finalize what I wanted to say. Sometimes it all takes place so fast that as soon as I can pick up a pen, it's written in my mind and flows right out, whole, onto the paper. I've typed poems into my laptop, flat in bed, barely awakened by the dream that wrote it.

I think everyone can write if they want to. At weddings and funerals, I've heard people stammer that they can't write, then proceed to read touching poems about their loved one. Put out the welcome mat for your feelings and write! It's super exciting to see what comes out. If you stifle something you think is unworthy, you may stop the flow of thoughts that lead to your very best. Let it all have its say! Here is a quaint example:

INSPIRATION: My dog had been desperately ill and my laundry was forgotten. Down to my last pair of clean undies, a silky pair I don't like, I felt them shift when I climbed in the car to go to my poetry sharing group. I thought, "Feels like I'm wearing someone else's underwear!" Four miles to town and the poem wrote itself on the way there. "Hells'a fun," is in memory of my dad; his phrase, "You kids got hells'a toys in the yard."

Shy Sister

Tonight, I'm wearing sister Sarah's underpants.
It's all that I can do to stay down off the bar,
I wanna dance!

I never should'a snuck this sexy bra
From sister Cass!
My Lord, I'm drinking beer!
And this is my 4th glass!

'N I can't help this walk
All bouncy, perky, twisty ...
Unknown to her, this dress I'm in
Belongs to sister Christy.

I've got my hand across my mouth,
Cause these are sister Patsy's shoes
I wanna grab that karaoke mic
And belt me out some blues!

I've never had so many men turn 'round
When I walk through a room!
'N all it took was one quick squirt
Of sister Violet's new Chanel perfume!

I've had me hells'a fun tonight,
I'm shy, as heaven knows!
When I go to the library next time at night
I'll be wearing my own clothes!

Crayons and Paint

Brief flashes of luminescent brilliance
Enclosed within mounds of muddy brown
Generous dollops of gray and black
Globs of nothingness white placed all around.

This is the palette of color that I was given
Assigned solely to its use to paint a life
Colors of distress, fear and boredom
Colors of despair, pain, grief, and strife.

Whatever, in heaven's name, was God thinking
I could create with such dull and listless hues?
Why not allow expanded color choices
Cerulean, magenta, sea foam, chartreuse?

Coveting paint boxes of all my kin and strangers
For years to come I'd whine, postpone, delay
I scarce came close to knowing my own colors
"I don't do crayons," I'd smirk and smartly say!

At last, when finally forced to start my painting
With little effort thoughtlessly succeeded
To paint myself into a corner cage
God knew this reverie was what was needed.

Forced to do nothing till that paint had dried
I viewed my palette now from angles all anew
When touched by light beams dancing from the sun
It flashed back purple, green, gold, red and blue.

Transfixed by richness newly there revealed
My guard dropped down and then came in the dawn
With help of light sent like a strobe from heaven
All those depressing hues seemed to be gone.

Others noticed me as they were passing near me
"Poor thing," I heard a thoughtless soul remark
"Trapped there with palette oh so bleak and gloomy
She'd be better off if it were total dark."

Like an age old gauntlet thrown into the ring
Stung by that slap, I sharply drew a breath
I may hate the lot I find that I've been given
But I'll defend my lot unto the very death.

God's purpose now revealed is thus cemented
I study my old palette now and muse
That contained within its dull and common colors
Lie the bases for a thousand brilliant hues.

I touch my palette now with great respect
Strengthened thus from this new point of view
I'll gladly take in hand my paint and crayons
And create beauty with these mighty few.

With frequent flashes of luminescent brilliance.

A nurse I had worked with for some time sat down and told me how much I bugged her. I was in charge, yet she was comfortable to express such annoyance with me? She meant it, too, but it was as refreshing as a spring rain to me. I broke into laughter. We talked about her perceptions of me. I learned leadership skills I needed. I grew.

Sometimes Life Requires a Second Look

Sometimes life is like a flower
We look at others lives and see
the lovely and bright
surface edges
and we think, Oh my! Wish my
life could be like that!
What we don't always notice is
the darkness that lies
behind the edge.
We don't always take into
consideration the deep despair
and loneliness
That may be the foundation for
the beauty we now see before us.

Often, the brightest days follow
the darkest stormy nights

and the most brilliant hues testify
of storm and searing heat
that worked together to bring
forth a perfect bloom.
Sometimes, life requires
a second look.

You are looking again
seeing beauty denied to your
eyes the first time around.
I am looking again and seeing
peace and safety
where I last saw judgment,
dissension and unhappiness.
I like how you have effected my
vision and how I have
effected yours.
I love you.

This is Patti Anne's saying. At first, I thought it was egotistical. Over time, I came to appreciate the importance of self-love, encouragement and celebration. She made it so much fun. Thank God for positive people. Double thank God for girlfriends!

Yay Me!

Dark red hair, find them everywhere
Good friends abound, my table surround
Accumulated treasures record my pleasures
The badges of full life is what I see. Yay me!

Red perfume scents the whole room
Mellow stereo, fragrant candle glow
Creating beauty from joy, not duty
The props I've chosen demonstrate my glee. Yay me!

Not illusion, solid conclusion
Action not reflection, avoiding introspection
My heart for hire, sit by my fire
I offer coffee royal and cups of tea
For I am Patti Anne! Yay me!

Long blond hairs on all of my chairs
Canned hair spray, everywhere spray
Talcum powder, fine dust clouder
The badges of my womanhood coat all I see. Yay me!

Chanel perfume fills the whole room
Romantic stereo, warm candle glow
Enhancing beauty, my natures' duty
The props I've chosen to sustain my glee. Yay me!

Mysterious illusion, feminine collusion
Mirrors reflection for self-inspection
When perfected, others selected
I can then offer wine and cups of tea.

For I am Bobbie Gayle! Yay me!

Life crises blend, welding friend to friend
Shared determination, resist extermination
Hope springs from stone, we are not alone
Together, we won't go down without a fuss
For we are friends supreme! Yay us!

The Aunties Card Game

Peas in a pod, these two are not
For one is moist and one is dry.
They share a passion . . .
playing cards
and never let a chance go by

Familiar scene to my small eyes,
the shuffler hums and riffles fast
and by some means . . .
they deal in turn
though days go by
since one dealt last.

They think I'm sleeping,
reading, bored
but I'm all ears and
watch these two!
Believe me, entertainment height
will be enjoyed
before they're through.

Aunt Rosie,
blond and plump and moist
lights up a cigarette and waits
as Auntie Lucy deals the cards
she calls for luck, to all the fates.

Aunt Lucy, lean and gray and dry
her knuckles crackle as she deals

and snaps the cards hard
on the deck
and counts each off,
till my head reels.

They murmur over every card
bemoan, rejoice, emotions show
But I soon learn to disregard
The gamesmanship is on, I know.

I focus on Aunt Rosie's joss
A chain that's filled
with lucky charms
A baby shoe, assorted keys
Green rabbit's foot
that met great harms.

Aunt Rosie drops the cards
like mud
I know who plays without a look
Aunt Lucy's style is crisp and dry
like someone slamming
shut a book.

Their jibes, their history,
family stuff
Flows like a stream
throughout their play
and I,
most favored child must be,
to be allowed to watch and stay!

Upon the Roof
With Shingles

A play on words this story
Of my bout with varicella.
While I wait deep in the night,
For drugs to take my pain away.

Visions marching in my mind
Entertain me in my stupor
I survey the hated trailing
Of this virus on display

Like a spotted leopard skin
Roseated footprints padding
Leaving supernumerary nipples
In a trail across my breast.

Memory of pleasures gone now
Just of sorrow from the searing
Like a range fed cow at branding
After red hot irons are pressed.

Branded by this phantom iron
An escapee from my child hood
I've got a photo of it somewhere
I've got proof I've had the Pox!

Taking out a tube of ointment
And assorted pills and capsules
I prepare to do my battle
Throwing wide my first aid box

In my velvet green pajamas
Hair cascading like a vision
Spatula and mirrors handy
Capsaicin is my recourse

I apply it to the sink bowl
I apply it to the counter
I apply it to my waistband
Why, oh why did I divorce?

All alone upon this roof top
One lone roofer for the mission
Overwhelmed to get it perfect
Pity makes my own soul pitch

Call it shingles, sounds so jolly
Hot as rooftops under noon sun
Scalding water splashed on skin
Burns like a howling, raging bitch.

Tried to count the syllables
While I am drunken from the
codeine.
Tried to make the rhythm work
Dress up all the salad words.

It's a wonder I can type this
So filled up with chemicals
Never mind the lack of sleeping
Shingles! Strictly for the birds.

I Am Wary Of The Winter

I am wary of the winter,
Of the darkness, of the cold
Of the stillness, so much quiet,
So alone, no one to hold

I am wary of the howling
Of the wind, when nights are long
Of the whisper of the ice cap
When she shifts and sings her song.

I am weary from the winter
Longing for the springtime thaw
When my heart will wake and listen
Then respond to new life's call.

I'll be weary from rejoicing
Digging in the fragrant soil
And I'll lay me down so peaceful
Tired from good and honest toil.

Yer Losin' Yer Cohesiveness, Girl!

What a beautiful composition of lies!
The life you'd long for; envy; kill for?
All held together with a fabulous glue,
called deception

I fooled me; forgot my true story
I fooled you;
put up quite the front, didn't I?
So some of you thought I was selfish
You were wrong, I was "shell-fish"
(as in empty shell, dearie)

Well, the glue is losing its cohesiveness, see?
The shell is slipping and I am no longer fooled.
You still don't believe the shell is not the real me
'cause you never knew me well anyway.
Even if you saw the deterioration of my world
and shouted
"Yer' losin' yer cohesiveness girl!"
I most likely would still lie to you
If you had perceived my plight
I may have let you in on the secret.

Thus,
it is up to me alone
to rearrange the pieces
and losing my cohesiveness
is a necessary part of the process.

Ashes to Dust to Woman

Ground to dust by the
heavy hand of hell
Blown to the four winds
Swept off the face of the earth
Dispersed into outer space.
Invisible to the naked eye
Yet reassembled in proper
alignment
One foot on Venus, one foot on
Saturn
I stood and viewed the universe
There in wonder I beheld the
Earth
With new vision, I saw my life as
it had been
And there, a change swept
through my being

No more was I the victim of
happenstance
The product of mores and
folkways
Of genetic code or even of
accidents
No more was I a childish female.

From that Far Vision place
I saw my life as a beautiful strand
Woven into the tapestry of time

Life unending, life connected to
the Eternal One
Life with purpose and
destinations.
Life not unnoticed nor forgotten.

Back in the here and now, I don
my veil,
Take a cleansing breath
And revisit that place, that vision.
Here and now, in the flesh
With my bones and blood attuned
to the heavens
I choose my steps and find my
paths
Struggling to become that
timeless creature again.

For I am a being of flesh
And I need to remind myself
That all is well, there are no
accidents
My comings and goings are
attended by the Ancient
And that I have bypassed the
bounds of hell
I need to remind myself that I am
eternal
And that
I AM WOMAN!

A Few Dollars and Sense

Always with me, close at hand
I keep myself a stash of dough.
Emergencies don't all need bills
But require sense to make them go.

Some $20s are the dollars
But the sense… there's more than five.
To start, a sense of gratitude
Thank God, I'm still alive!

There's second-sense, that woman thing
And sense of decency
My favorite … sense of humor
Helps me keep my sanity.
My sense of time, too often flawed
Assailed by sense of pressing needs
That mother's sense that lingers on
Sniffs out when trouble sows her seeds.

Miss Common Sense must reign supreme
She sorts out chaos close at hand
Sense of direction points the way
To make a wise and righteous stand.

And standing guard with sense of pride
And steady sense of loyalty,
The sense of right and wrong assist
Make sense of nonsense that I see.

Expectation

Expectation,
A game I choose no longer play.
Chomping, waiting for "that" day.
Expectation
A dream I set that must come true
Some silent debt I lay on you.

Expectation
Sets the end before the story
Demanding hoped and longed for glory
Expectation
Best be cured by patient repose
Awaiting destiny to disclose

Expectation
To God now bow and give control
And trust the peace that rests my soul.
Patience
The cure for expectations
I rest my machinations

Patience
Will be her own sweet reward
Bringing peace and not a sword.
Patience
Says I choose to live in trust
Brushing off the years of dust.

A Thousand Tiny Lights

You tossed my soul
clear and pure
like a delicate crystal globe

In my mind's eye
I watched it arc up
followed its descent,
saw it crash
against the brick wall
of your indifference

I counted
a thousand tiny lights
each glowing brightly,
sending out
an S.O.S signal
like a homing beacon

And incredibly
realigning
linked
into a useful network
toning, humming
the same phrase
Save Our Selves

Adventures Recalled

Rotten fences
Weed-grown crossing
Magic meadow
Baseball tossing

Naked swimming
Dammed up creek.
Grapevine gully
Swing all week.

Big tall oak tree
Secret clubhouse.
Secret password
Something meese mouse

Oft remembered
childhood places
Now hold strip mall
Parking spaces.

Age and Wisdom

Age and wisdom don't equate
Nor guarantee the other
I thought the opposite was true
but was I wrong? Oh brother!

A blooming woman, seeking both,
when I observed this truth:
Some adults act most foolishly
both hasty and uncouth.

I've tried to learn how God expects
wise humans to behave.
And pray to be most wise and old
before I hit my grave.

Be Uncomforted!

Hopes and dreams achieved
may be celebrated in comfort
but don't stay there!

In comfort we
become complacent,
compliant!
Vision dulls and
freedom ebbs away!
Past victories become insignificant
as the world beats a path
around our drive-way!
Kingdoms are lost in comfort!

Be uncomforted!
Find a pea or a pebble
of a thought,
a cause, a hope
a dream, a need
to lie on;
to keep you awake
aware alive and moving
thinking doing;
changing rearranging
recreating the old
into better things
Progress arrives
On the tide of discomfort.

An About Face, The Bug Poem

What do I abhor
For ever and more
Above thugs?
  Bugs!

What doth complain
'Neath my window pane
Spurning yon thicket?
  The cricket!

Who, though unseen
Doth sneak through my screen
To hunt fruit or fat
  The gnat!

And stealing life's juice
Himself so to spruce
That skinny bandito
  Mosquito!

His erratic flight
I watch day and night
Lest he land in my pie
  The Fly!

With much speed he crawls
In corners and walls
That old cobweb rider
  The spider!

When he makes his habitat
Within my cabinat (I can do it if
Ogden Nash can)
In rage I approach
  The Roach!

Once tender I felt
As observing, I knelt
But love now I can't
  Any ant!

No longer a mouse
I fight for my house
The best friend I've made?
  RAID!

GIRLS TALK ABOUT ANGER

I shared my poetry by shipping it in Bcc email to a list of 100+ friends. Far and away the topic that brought the most feedback was anger. That's why I wrote the poem, "Not Everything I Write Is About Us," which I included in the Introduction. The response was so interesting to me though, that I wrote several more poems about anger.

The first of the three poems that follow came to mind when I asked myself, "How mad was she?" It was written just so I could use the line, "Flies wouldn't light on her!"

Pressure Properly Applied

I tell ya, I don't know when I ever
saw anybody so mad!
Madder'en Hell's Hounds she was!
Madder'en a hen house
fulla wet cluckers!
I thought her head was gonna
blow clean off!

Old men quaked in their shoes
Stray dogs ran the other way
The leaves trembled
and fell off the trees
Birds left the berry bushes
hangin' full.
I even slunk away
and hid under the porch.
Flies wouldn't light on her!

Stomping' them stubby legs
she marched
Her bumbershoot
clutched like a club!
The path cleared before her
like a tidal wave!

You could feel it, taste it,
smell it ...

ANGER - PURE -
UNADULTERATED - ANGER
Anger right outta her soul, tight,
stomped down hard
'N turned right into crystal rage...
Like she'd been storin' it
for centuries.
I can see it clear...years of
aggravation and grief and
disappointment.
All tamped down and brewin'
out of sight

Kinda reminds me of something
I read once
about how coal is formed.
All that organic muck under all
that incredible pressure
But give it some more pressure
and give it some more time
An' man, you got a diamond!
Ain't nothin' prettier, colder,
sharper or tougher than a
diamond!

Things ain't been the same 'round
here since that day, I can tell ya!
Very, very inneresten'!

Belly Full of Anger

Whazzat? No, Honey,
I aint pregnant!
I jist gots me a belly fulla anger
underneath this shirt!

Looks like a watermelon I figger
from out there.
but the way I sees it
it's more like a giant Easter Egg

Whazz in it, y'all ask??
Well, Sugar, thass fer me to know
an fer me to fine out.
So HANDS OFF, its mine!
Doan'chew even think about it!

Ennyways. I been carrying
this load alone
For so damn long.
an' yew don't need to know
what's in it!

Maybe some of yer own
ol' rotten egg anger
you spilled out all over me!
Maybe thass what's in it!

I aim to open this baby
when'em damn good'n ready.
Kinder got ust to carryin' it.

Enny how, I still got them
other eggs
Y'all know, the ones y'all like.
Them hollow chocolate ones
Cuvverd with fancy foil

An' them other'ns, y'all know.
marshmallow'n cuvverd
with stuff.
pink n purple sugar 'n other
sweet shit.
This here big ol sucker
is all mine!

A Pocket Full of Anger

Sing a song of six pence
A pocketful of rye.
When I touch my anger
I begin to cry.

Tip toe, tip toe, here come the anger men.
Climbing up my throat and choking down again.
Now they make my heart ache
And make my jaw get tight
I want to spit them out before another anger night.

Hi diddle diddle, the cat played the fiddle
the truth went over the moon
I danced as I stuffed it
The whipped puppy swallowed
But it's coming back up really soon.

Pussy cat, pussy cat, where have you been?
I've been in hiding to cover my scream.
Pussy cat, pussy cat, what did you there?
I was the frightened mouse under a chair.

Don't Be Afraid,
I Won't Hurt You!

Don't be afraid, I won't hurt you!
I am love.
Give of me freely
and I will come back to you.
But just by giving
you will be blessed
beyond measure.

Don't be afraid, I won't hurt you!
I am anger.
I show you where
your boundaries lie.
In this way, I help protect you.
Use me wisely and
you will be strengthened.

Don't be afraid, I won't hurt you!
I am fear.
I show you where you need
faith and wisdom,
but don't let me drive
for I will make you lose your way.

Don't be afraid, I won't hurt you!
I am courage.

I reside in the core of your being
and it is I
who makes you step forth boldly
into the battles of life.
I am the very flame of desire
for life and for living.

Don't be afraid, I won't hurt you!
I am simply a feeling
an emotion.
I am not you.
I do not define you.
I am simply your servant.

Don't be afraid, I won't hurt you!
But do look at me
examine me.
Say, "Love is present
and it feels wonderful."
Say, "Anger is present,
how can I use it wisely?"
Say, "Hmm, fear is present,
what is it I am to learn?"
Say, "Courage is present.
Oh, how I love being alive!"
I am life!
Don't be afraid, I won't hurt you!

In the span of my lifetime, the next two subjects have truly come out of the closet. Women share, but so do men. The research into PTSD with helpful therapies, and finally, some serious legal action, has given hope to many. Still, the tide of victims floods and stains our society.

Hats off to a beloved friend who sent her father-in-law to prison to protect her children. Accolades to so many people I've known who did the difficult work of facing their fears and doing the healing. Sympathy and understanding to so many more who choose to keep their secrets, rather than face being further victimized by families and communities who are unbelieving, unsupportive and blaming.

Funny Uncles

We call them "Funny Uncles"
But they're really rotten churls.
Those who take their sexual pleasure
From little boys or girls.

They think we won't remember
We're so young that we'll forget
They buy us toys and presents
Instill fear to hedge their bet.

When they finally get exposed
The fools don't plead insanity
"That was so long ago,"
they whine,
"and it was she who seduced me."

"You know she was so clinging
She danced standing on my feet
Consent was truly mutual
When I took her offer sweet."

Don't forget I was just seven
And you, maybe twenty-three
When you brought your evil to me
Stole my sense of purity.

You say I acted sexy
Normal growth accounts for that
You the adult, me the child
and you're just talking through your hat.

You're blackballed from the family
So pack your bags to go.
There's new innocence among us
Like you don't all ready know.

Those of us who can, now tell it
We have named your name out loud
We refuse to let you prey now
Getting lost in some new crowd.

The gendarmes here to take you
Soon you'll have a new address
At our local county prison
Better take along a dress.

They don't like your kind inside there
At least that's what we all hear.
You'll be branded
"Sexual Predator"
If you do get out some year.

I've no pity for you, Uncle.
Your fate's just a puny span,
Those you touched and victimized
They would forget, but never can.

For the damage lasts a lifetime
Scars inside that can't be seen
Twist in ways so unexpected
We feel alone and so unclean.

Nothing's funny about these uncles.
If a list of names was made
Would someone you know be on it?
For fear alone, it's often stayed.

Not Documentable!

They said they cannot document
Abuse like I've been through
Can't photograph my shattered soul
They'd like a bruise or two.

Unprovable! Your word alone …
We just can't act on that
Could you have misconstrued intent?
Straight face, their eyes don't bat.

Good God Almighty! Are you daft?
My will is not my own!
He's taken everything from me.
I have no car, no phone!

It was so subtle, this decline
I'm not a stupid girl!
I knew some bruisers, long ago,
Didn't see his flag unfurl.

No, this was different, this was love
We planned a life together
Our sun was bright, and things were good …
Till we hit stormy weather.

Anticipate the end of this?
Oh, honey, let me tell!
While I was sick and in my bed
My life became pure hell.

Passive aggressive was his style
Yes, yes, I'll get your pills.
Day after day he put it off
And me with fever chills.

Confined, cut off, no mercy near
He looked into my eye
Declared, "You know, for my sake
'twould be best if you'd just die.

And so he fed me tainted food
On soapy coated plate
With folded arms, watched
while I retched
Like clay, molding my fate.

And yes, he hit me, hurt me bad
But never left a mark
So strange, left my computer
My companion in the dark.

Thank God for caring strangers
There online, he couldn't see
Identifying dangers
Making calls to get me free.

Not documentable they said
When rescue came my way.
I left behind all that I had
But I'm alive today.

So let me document for you
Abuse won't always show.
Eroded love can turn to hate
Can kill you, steady, slow.

If your own soul is shrinking
From a separated life …
Cut off from work, from family
More slave than lover, wife

Cut loose, get gone! Run!
Save yourself!
Just take what you can carry
Cause documentable's too late …
When it's your obituary.

Behave or I'll Kick Your Ass

Don't give me no lip
'n don't give me no guff
I come from the south
don't put up with that stuff.

No wise acre comments
and none of your brass
If you get out of line
I'll be kicking your ass.

It's for your own good, now,
so no whiney noise
or your ass will get kicked
by some REAL good ol boys.

I Accept

I accept you and your way of life
I accept me, the way I
choose to go
I accept that there's great variety
and none's to say which is
the better show.

I accept that every soul
must choose
Which way to walk, to talk,
to worship, and believe
But what I find
most bitter to accept
Is that you hear my view, frown,
turn and leave.

You Will Lose Me

If you choose contention
At the slightest mention
You will lose me.

If you create strife
As your way of life
I will be gone.
If you gain your ground
Grinding others down
I cannot be near you.

If you choose love
Compassion
Flexibility
Show the slightest effort at understanding the gifts within your trials
Seeing a bigger picture, as if viewing them from the moon
Cast the slightest shadow of releasing debts of anger and grief
Grasp the ability to turn your back and face the other way
State an intention to move from your wounded state
Inviting the spirit of forgiveness to nest in your heart
Seeking to grow instead of shrink
Then I can bear to stay.

I will have peace, love, joy, hope, surrounding me.
It is my birthright.
Gaining it is my choice.

Can't Figger' You Out

When I look at you so quiet
Don't suspect that I might be
Tryin' how to figger' you out
Cause I'm looking in at me.

I don't want to be intrusive
To your sacred holy space
What you see is signs of listenin'
Etched right there upon my face.

I'm so hoping as you're sharing
There is wisdom at your knee
And I'm watching
While you're speaking
For mirrored images of me.

How you take me is important
How I take you, just to learn
And I take you as you are, friend
Take me that way in return.

I don't stuff you in compartments
Or presume to know you better
Than you know your own
true spirit
(That one rates a
"Dear John" letter.)

Let's just spend some
time together
As we laugh and play a while
Scoping out the joy in living
With no smug or knowing smile.

If I tried to slot and file you
And your every nuance sift
I would miss your
unique presence
And your trust, your dearest gift.

GIRLS TALK ABOUT LOVE

Girls Will Talk

While growing up, I was so good
For fear the boys would talk
And none would ever pick me out
To take that wedding walk.

Much older now, much freer too,
I see the tables turned.
For girls talk freely of their men
And how they've gotten burned.

Who snores and belches,
has bad breath
Who's skimpy with his shower
Cause girls talk in the rest rooms
It's been told within the hour.

If you're a drunk,
a cheapskate, well …
it's known all over town
Cause girls in beauty parlors
Love to cut those guys
right down.

And if your conversation is
Me, mine, myself alone,
With no regard for her thoughts,
well …
Girls share that on the phone.

Behaviors, mannerisms are
Observed with critic's eye
And girls talk in their kitchens
Serving guys up just like pie!

I'm Done With Men!

I made a vow!
I'm done with men.
Unless ...
he likes to hear me talk
To hear my thoughts
and thinks me wise
For him
I might try men again.

I'm much too old
To fool around with men
Unless ...
he traces fingers
Down my face my neck
And tilts my chin
For him
I might try men again.

I've seen too many men!
I'm through!
Unless ...
he sees me too
And looks into my soul
For him
I might try men again.

It's too much work!
I'm done with men.
Unless he likes to do things
Side by side, a team
And tilts my chin
And thinks me wise
And looks into my eyes.
For him
I might try men again.

Birds of Prey

Thoughts of romance
Like birds of prey
Circle round us
Ready to pounce

Hungry, hungry
Wanting feeding
Devouring friendship
By priceless ounce.

Wary, cautious
Thinkers, we
Eye those vultures
Toss a crumb.

Preserve the loaf
Lest it be spoiled
And leave us barren
Starved and numb.

The Cost of Loving

If sweet and good or foul with rot
Oh dear, I fear
It costs the same no matter what.
You thought it free,
the gift of love?
Oh no, not so

(A spotless lamb,
a pure white dove.
Your firstborn child,
your restful night
The single bulb you have for light
Your last three coins,
the crust of bread
That stands between you
and the dead.)

Is it fair gain, this fee that's laid?
Oh yes, I guess
And every cent sure to be paid.

When love goes bad,
the wound is deep
It's strife for life!
You stumble, limp,
moan in your sleep.

But when love's good,
exquisite pains
Yes indeedy, sweetie
Hellos, good byes,
love song refrains.

Two legs or four,
your heart is chained
Oh my, we'll cry
Worry and grief
can't be contained.

And those well loved
whose dreams are lost
Those near and dear
You'll bleed for them,
unending cost.

I Cannot Save You

Hey look here, I'm just a woman
And I'm broken deep inside
I have run from you, avoiding
Now I've got no place to hide.

I've no time to help you, Sugar
I'm too busy saving me
Please don't rock my boat so fierce
Lest we both tumble in the sea!

I am old, too old, too tired
Do not think that I would do
And I'm fearful of your needing
Don't trust me to love you true.

I have longed to find a strong man
Who will make my life of ease
Give me comforts for my late years
Let me do just as I please.

If it's saving that you're needing
Then best look some other way
For I quit the saving business
And I'm open just to play.

If I Fall In Love

If I fall in love
will I still be able to walk
on the Earth?
Or will I float right off
as soon as love gives birth?

If I fall in love
will I be pulled down
underneath some tide of pain
and have to sink or swim
all on my own again?

If I fall in love at all
will I survive the landing?

These thoughts close in mind
why would one choose a fall
as a means of entering
Into such a thing as love at all?

An Ovarian Encounter

Hello and Holy God!
I thought you girls were dead!
Where you been for all these years?
N'why choose now to raise your head?

You say you've got a yen?
Bad Boy has touched your moon?
You've lit your candles for him
Hoping he'd be coming soon?

You're burning up MY jeans!
You're messing with MY sleep
You know how hard I tried, but
He's not into us that deep.

So sorry, sisters dear,
Resume your pelvic rests
You'll know if he approaches
By carillons from our breasts.

Love Sick

I am sick from love
and afraid there is no cure
And why am I sick?
How is it that love
can make me sick?
Sick love makes me sick!

Sick love:
Love with a price tag
Love with chains
Love that drains from secret expectation
Love that locks me in a mold
Love with a foot on my throat
Love that feeds on my soul
and does not feed me back.

What's this?
You say there's a cure?
I'm calling the doctor right now!

Miss Gayly's Rampage

Evur Saturday night
It's the same daggone thang
Them cowboys ride ryat into town.
They lean on the wall
At the local dance hall
Jist chuggin them cold beers ryat down.

Evur Saturday night
All the girls gits dressed up
Cuz' they wun'nt pass up enny chance
They head fer the hall
Like some fancy dress ball
All they got in thar head's is to dance.

Evur Saturday night
It's the same daggone show
Them fellers jis gawks at thu gurls
They talk 'bout their trucks
How they shoot does 'n bucks
But choosin' no partners for whirls.

Well last Saturday night
Miss Gayly come into town
And she's madder'n enny wet hen
"Them fellers don't dance
Jist prospectin' our pants
An this dosi-do's jist bout to en'."

What a Saturday night!
She stood ryat on that floor
Her Ladysmith clutched in her hands
Shot clean through the roof
"Cowpokes hit the hoof!
Ain't gonna be no one-nyght-stands!"

Evur Saturday night
When the cowboys come now
Everbuddy will find their bryght star
An' it's thanks to Miss Gayle
With her rampagin' wail
"Don't dance? Get the hail outta' my bar!"

Oh, Let Me Down Easy

Oh, let me down easy
Don't drop me and run
Don't burn me to cinders
Like a blast from the sun

Oh, let me down easy
I'm soft and I'm sore
From the dozens of falls
I have taken before.

Oh, let me down easy
With words that say why
Please don't walk away
Without saying goodbye.

Oh, let me down easy
My heart's bound to break
If another harsh blow
From a love it must take.

Oh, let me down easy
I'll just walk away
I won't stay and whimper
Naming debts you must pay.

Oh, let me down easy
I will be able then
To keep holding up high
both my head and my chin.

Captive In Your Silence

Anticipating some word of hope
I hang about in your presence, waiting
God forbid my attention waver
for even so much as a second.
The longed for, watched for encouragement
is not forthcoming and I may as well
be surrounded with bars.

Are you unaware or did you plan?
Such as the case may be, I see now,
that you're holding me to you,
captive, in your silence

Rainbow On the Water

The girl is shallow, the girl is sick
She has the depth of an oil slick
I'm not talking Exxon Valdez, no way!
But something on the order
of Pam aerosol spray.

Oh, she had a lot of glitter
like some much sought after gold,
but when your sun went down, son
she was shallow, cruel and cold.

So remember son, when looking for
what will fulfill your life,
better lay her by a yard stick
E're you say '"Please be my wife!"

Cause not every rainbow anchors
down inside a pot of gold,
and it takes a little time son,
for the full truth to unfold.

Not every rainbow signals
this is God's own gift to you
But there's one out there a'looking
hoping she'll find one like you!

This next poem sounds rather self indulgent,
but it's a common story told when young or old
girlfriends gather and pour out their hearts.
Most girls (and guys) don't want to sit in
the ugly trap called "the buddy seat."

One Hopes

That one's intoxicating beauty
steady love and devotion
will capture the fancy
of one's desired objective.
And that one's devastating wit and wisdom
Will latch said target with total devotion
magnetically, magically
to a place of honor within it's space
Reciprocating the magical, magnetic beauty
that the presence of love generates.

One hopes
In light of common hopes and interests
That one will see reciprocal love blossom
On that targeted face.

Oh, sadness
Upon realizing one's folly.
When comes the dawning that the one hoped for
Has found another target, which got there first
And with intoxicating magnetism
And devastating wit and beauty
drew forth the love that appeared briefly
on that face as he expounds on love.
And as it flickers and flares into full flame
the target for which he aims
flicks that love away like a mosquito

She sees the love, the devotion and the pain
and blows it away
with the casualness of a child
poofing a ripened dandelion into the wind.

The unlucky one arriving late,
now serving as leaning post
as sounding board and as witness ... a buddy
to the destruction of that dream.
Eventually, one learns
that love is like a magnetic door latch
attracting not only it's intended target
but also any free metallic crumbs
that stray into it's field of influence.

A pity, really, what a body learns from hoping.
But good friends can be made that way.
One should always hope think carefully,
before jumping in
and making a total fool of themselves

Spoon Feeding the Rattlesnake

Your friends say you are worth it
And the effort I should take
But they warn to take it easy
Like you'd feed a rattlesnake.

Quite a picture, I'm not foolish
Haven't got the proper spoon
So I'm backing off real quickly
Let no snake get near me soon.

I'm not desperate for a fella
Sure not one who is thus coiled
That with inadvertent movement
My good health could be despoiled.

Go and eat your mice and slither
To some other hunting ground
There's no chance I'll use my silver
For one who strikes with rattle sound.
Hmmmmm …
He was more like a Fer-de-Lance, actually.

Grapefruit Guys

Around they roll, just as they please
Not easy then to stop their spin.
Juice up the places where they play,
but never really let you in. Sin!

Once past the peel, the pith the pits
The taste invigorates the buds.
But there's more waste, than what you ate
Commitment wise, these guys are duds!

Still, tempting is forbidden fruit
Perhaps it's worth the effort then,
If you've a certain lust for life,
To get beneath this fellow's skin.

Such juicy, fragrant, tasty fruit!
He's sure a top-ten hitter
He brings it all: the sweet, the tart
but most of all the bitter.

The Men Who Put Up Walls

Here's to the men who put up walls
To keep the women out!
Those walls are like magnetic bait
And women stand and pout

And nearly every one of them
Is sure she has the stuff
To tear that wall down brick by brick
And tame that wild man gruff.

So with a vengeance they do climb
And hit a mighty lick
And many find to their despair
The wall is just too thick.

Not all that's wild needs to be tamed
Nor all that's hidden, found.
Best not to scale those mighty walls
To tumble to the ground.

Here's to the men whose walls are thin
With doors and windows too
With eyes that look to see who's there
Discerning false from true.

Here's to those women, rarest breed
Their wisdom legendary
Who by their love and faithfulness
Make walls unnecessary.

Oh, Shit, I Think I'm In Love

Oh, shit, I think I'm in love
and I didn't mean to be.
You will have to hog tie me, my sweet,
to drag me to admission, submission.
I don't know when
I have ever felt such fear.

I am in over my head, drowning in it
drunk in it, sick in it.
Out of control, not a bad thing
Out of resistance, used it up trying
fighting it, weakening
Come and take me away!

E-Mail Lover

A name in my In-box
A voice on the phone.
Though often agreeing
There's no sense of home.

Ah, something is missing
Connection I need
Some sense of a lover
My longing to feed.

If you were as caring
With love as with work
You wouldn't leave women
Calling you Mr. Jerk.

Oh, that is my cursing
This vision so deep
That I see within you
A boy fast asleep.

Oh, what happened to you?
What wounded you so
When love makes appearance
You pack up and go?

If you wrote a contract
Just how would it read?
"You wait, little woman
Till I feel a need!

Like Rapunzel, stay put
In a tower with no stair
Until I come to visit
Let none visit there!"

So I'll be your pen-pal
And chat like old friends
But I won't be grieving
When this chapter ends.

Want Me? You Can't Have Me!

Braided hair, freckles, glasses
skinny little girl in school.
All you fellows liked to taunt me
took my books,
you were so cruel.

Now I look like Christie Brinkley
Pamela A. and Vanna White
Guess you never thought
I'd fill out!
Guess what?
You did not think right.
Trim and golden, long blond hair
Breasts that make you salivate
Have no tan line you can see
Want me?
Don't you even think to wait.

Rightly I'm described
as gorgeous,
rich as sin, smart as a whip.

I read those books
you wouldn't carry!
Want me? You're on shore,
I'm on the ship.

Should have listened
to the pastor
naughty, nasty boys so free.
Running roughshod over others
Now you want,
but you can't have me!

I am a woman of distinction
and I closely guard my gate
If you dream
you'll share my fortunes
Forget it fella, you're too late!

I'll go alone throughout my life.
By choice, alone most willingly
Unless you too
have been transformed
and are an equal match for me.

Within the Emptiness, I Felt You Coming to Me

Alone!
Sick of it
Filled to over full with it
Determined to outwit it
Alone, I waited
Alone in that empty space.

From across the universe
I felt your approach.
Trees began to sway
Birds left their nests,
swirling up in a spiral dance,
settling down again around me.
The air became heavy, pulling at me,
stealing my breath away.
Barely able to think, to stand, to walk
I waited and marveled …
Nothing was as it had been.
Nothing was familiar
It was all so very strange
but I knew to listen, be alert, be ready.
I knew
something incredible, unstoppable, irresistible
was roaring across the universe in my direction
And it was love
And it was you.

My life will never be the same again
nor would I want it thus,
for I love you so.

He Is the One! He Is the One!

Wandering down the years since then
I found companions time, again
And told myself, though poised to run
He is for fun! He is for fun!

Now comes a man, unlike the rest.
Who's drawn from me, my very best
My joyful heart cry has begun
He is the one! He is the One!

Tsunami

Tidal wave
of great proportion
sweeping all before it
dismantling what hands
have constructed
leaving only that
raw material
from which
we spring

Tsunami
a sweeping rush of emotion
that overturns and dismantles
what I thought I believed
altering my inner landscape
forevermore.

Tsunami's
of love and of tenderness
strip my heart of pretense
neutralize my defenses
negate my fearfulness
Leaving me in
a space surreal
where sound cannot penetrate
unable to speak
unable to walk

I see your lips move
I hear no words
I turn toward the sun
and feel no heat
somewhere between earth
and sky
I am held in thrall
and only the wash
of this tidal wave
connects my mind
and body.

Tsunami
has come upon me
and I am not
here anymore
I am gone
Soon to reappear
in some new form
in some new fullness.
Reconstructed
Filling up a gentler frame.

And I have Loved you

I have loved you although
I barely knew you
your history,
a mystery
not yet read.

Yet I have loved you
as if we've always
been together
our hearts now beat
as knit by common thread

So closely knit
that on examination
impossible to see
one end and one begun.

Our love a metronome
to pace the pulsing
our hearts keep time
in rhythm beat as one.

My eyes in comfort
look upon your face
as if we've always
known each other
old friends,
who happily share space.

We laugh
Oh, how we laugh
at us, deep belly stuff
the kind that spirits mend

And that alone assures me
we're not mad
we still possess our wits
we make a superb blend

I have loved you as if we
were conjoined spirit twins
who long ago
were pulled apart to bits
and now rejoined, I'm loving you
because this is a love
that truly fits
and I have loved you.

GIRLS TALK ABOUT BREAKING UP

How Am I to Trust You?

How am I to trust you,
that you love me?
You have broken something
delicate and precious.
A love that grew from years
of loving and sharing.

And that you willingly shattered it,
methodically and analytically
having determined on your own
that there was something better;
that your chances looked better
for happiness in the future with her
than with me?

You weren't even careful
but commanded me to stay away,
depending on my obedience
born from years of my trusting you,
being co-operative,
to hide your tracks.

And now you ask me to trust again?

I Never Loved You!

I never loved you! Never!
My heart never skipped a beat
Never dropped down to my feet!
Never!
I never loved you! Never!
My throat never closed in thrall
When you came in sight at all!
Never!
I never loved you! Never!
My eyes never shed a tear
When you walked away from here
Never?

The Most Ridiculous Thing

It was the most ridiculous thing I ever heard
And it struck me then as painfully absurd
Un-churched, he wished he was a Mormon man
So he could have two wives, like some Mormons can.

I wasn't laughing, this was way beyond funny
To hear this man whom I had known as "Honey"
When caught with his little "side-dish" pigeon
Try pacifying me, by bringing up religion.

No Relationship

"No relationship is better
than a bad relationship,"
A wise man said to me.
And he should know,
he had his share
of the bad ones, two or three!

I stood and mused upon his plight,
and thought perhaps that I
could be the one to bring him good
Yeah, right! In some pig's eye!

The man was superficial,
egotistic to a fault.
No riches from my goodness
could find home in his heart's vault.

But his advice is worthy,
though my hopes of love grow dim,
cause I'd rather have myself alone
than to be hooked up with him!

Hot Dog Man

He was slick and nearly hairless,
that man I loved
who left me blue,
so I squirted him with mustard
when he told me
we were through!

I shudder now just thinking
of his skin so smooth and slick.
Remembering how I trusted him
makes me equally as sick.

Now I'm repelled by hairless men
whose bodies sweat and shine,
like hot dogs lined up on a grill
at the fair summer time.

Give me a bald and burly guy
who grows his crop of hair
on chest and arms and back
and legs
and a beard way down to there.

I love the feel of facial hair
that rubs against my face
or strokes my skin with purpose
tickling every tender place.

Unlike the slimy feel of sweat
that's left by hot dog men,
who pull you close and moisturize
from your toes up to your chin.

To cuddle with a fuzzy man
is one of life's great joys!
Androgynous in every way,
spare me those waxed-off boys!

My ode to hair is quite sincere,
I'm kidding not at all!
Man, you gotta look like
Smokey Bear
if you're giving me a call!

Woman Without A Country

From far away
and long ago
I've come
across the barrens
where no green thing grows.
The memories gone of who I am
or who I was,
from whence I came

A woman without a country
longing to come home.
Lacing my shoes
picking up my walking stick
and on the trail again.

I've Not Been Touched for Eons

I'm alone and
I've not been touched for eons.
No familiar pat
No stroking of my hair
No fiddling with my thumbs
No brush of soft exhale on my neck
No lover's lips on mine
No glance locked into my eyes
Caressing my heart and soul
I have not been touched for eons
My very skin weeps.

Vicious Circles

I call it sick, that desperate love
That holds a thorn to quickly shove
into the healing, wounded heart
lest what was joined not stay apart

If all we've known in life is pain
we will know fear when peace we gain
The place such pain takes in a life
becomes quite dear, a husband, wife.

Pain gave to us identity
so we feel lost when we're pain free.
A twisted view, we've come to know.
Temptation screams, this peace hurts so

I have no sense who I might be
unless some pain resides in me.
Give me that thorn! Pain fix I need
or I'll be lost and can't proceed!

Thus do we circle round and round
Till comfort in the calm is found.
In patterns thus we make our trails
Break them we must or healing fails.

The Scenario

He is so full of life.
He makes her think.
She pursues him.
She realizes his slipperiness.
She backs off, enjoying him occasionally.
Creates much pain for herself in longing.

He finds "real woman."
She makes him think.
Adds her to his harem as a "visiting star."
Finds her to be slippery.
Cannot determine what he wants.
It's the closest he's ever been to being in love.
Scary.
Sees her slip away as he ponders safety
in familiar past loves.

Treading the Re-Birth Waters

I'm treading water
Hoping folks don't notice
I'm about to drown
I hate making a scene
But I hate this chaos!

My life used to be simple once
I think maybe
I want this all to end
and orderliness to be in place

I despair when I think how it was
I can't go back to that apathy
I want to go ahead to newness
I want to be alive, lively.

There are dragons on the road
Aloneness … separateness
I feel so naked … vulnerable
Unattached … uncared for.

Still looking for the security
of the womb?
Oh, it's secure all right
That prison where you are
sheltered, fed
and limited in growth!

The keeper doesn't have
total control,
Systems aren't perfect
Babies die there sometimes,
you know.
They tangle in their cords
and smother,
asphyxiated by their own actions.

Think!
Is that a reason
to not choose life again?
Or a reason to resolve
To leave the womb
and make it on your own?

Totally Enough!

I am broken up, beaten down, dazed
Maybe like a war survivor.
Surely to God you don't expect such people
To have a heart for "intimate, meaningful exchange."

"Total caring - Total sharing"
Is too little, too late for our past
Too much, too soon for our now.
And a bid you make, for me to share my diary.

Total caring? Look at me! Listen!
I say ENOUGH!
You keep on talking.
You, who eats and eats
but can't be filled.
Though you have nibbled away nearly all of me.

Two have become one: you.
But there is just enough of me remaining
To say, ENOUGH!!! I'm totally outta' here.

Off With the Costumes

He begs for reconciliation.
I can't bear to look at him.
I peek. I feel not much.
I can't wait to leave his presence.
It's not the same "uncomfortable" I was before.
Then I couldn't bear to look at the mirror;
Couldn't bear to see what he represents to me.

I see grass turf, rolled over hard, dry clay.
I see a thoroughbred suit, draped over a donkey.
I see an "End of the Line" sign
at mid-point of a round trip.
I see the Dead Sea.

I look at me and know these things are there:
The emptied spirit, covered with facade.
I see how I had laid down in the crypt
To die? No. To exist by choice, from fear.
I see my desire to move and go climb
stopped by my shroud of "You aren't strong enough."

I see the riches
The concentrated wealth of years of inflow
collected in that "dead sea"
And know it could be tapped.

It could flow out
If I can love myself.

I see endings, final decisions.
I want openings, new beginnings.

The prospect of returning to the marriage
Which I cherished and tended for so long
Has no appeal.
Have we reversed positions?
Me, distant and "right"
Him, clinging, forgiving, hoping
Silently bleeding internally?

I will find where the ending began.
Where the cessation of caring first budded
As the first primordial slime
produced the "spark of life"
this ending had a beginning too.
It was the fluke, the final lightning bolt
That lit the sequence to set it off.
Ah, too much struggle.
I can't face such a challenge right now.
Fuck the marriage.
I served it well but it is cracked.
Like Humpty Dumpty.

Gettin' By

I am surely a wondrous thing
Held together with gum and with string.
A patch holding in what is left of my brain
Wire wrapped all around is withstanding the strain.

But it works.

Whatever it takes me to stay on my feet
I don't even care if it's matching and neat
Cause to bloom and shine in this life is my goal
And to fan the bright spark of my God given soul.

And it works.

I hobble along at persistent snail's pace
And I plaster a positive smile on my face.
There's a whole lot of truth in that P.M.A. stuff
(As a life-long ambition it isn't enough)

But for right now, it works.

What the Hell Were You Thinking?

You can't enclose a wire in glass
And create a little light.
So detractors told Tom Edison
Who took the darkness from the night.

You can't take water out of wine
You're really not that handy,
Traditionalists told the clever Dutch
Who went on to create Brandy.

You'll never make that crate stay up
Pooh-pooh-ers told the Wrights.
Now we praise their bold invention
On trans-continental flights.

You cannot live without me, girl
You'll fall flat on your face.
But I've gone alone on happy trails
And of you there's not one trace.

What in hell were you thinking,
All you folks who pour on strife?
When we, the brave adventurers
Dared to bring our dreams to life?

I Dreamed

I dreamed of excrement last night!
Great prize winning, eye popping
sausages of brown!

I watched in amazement
as the giants stir and swirl
and then flush down.

I feel emptied, cleansed
Rid of useless leavings
I've let go this harbored shit of life

No more I'll hold it close
try to assimilate it, that stuff retained
that's cut me like a knife.

There's something miserly within
when constipated … with old pain
Unlikely sign of small and grasping mind

Best let it go along its way
the offal of the past
and with lightened step move on,
and ne'er again rebind.

Vacation With My Ex. Taking Stock. Summing Up.

I've been in your presence
Lo, these many quiet miles
Sharing sudden lightened laughter
exchanging fleeting, knowing smiles.
And yes, we have attained a level
long forged comfort, it is true
but there's nothing left between us
nothing left I want from you.
It is really and truly over.

GIRLS TALK ABOUT PARENTING

Possibly you recall Ann Landers' newspaper advice column. In 1975-76, she conducted a poll asking, "If you had it to do over, would you have children." An astounding 70% of her respondents, 80% of them women, voted "No!" Many of those related details to explain, confessing these were things they never verbalize to a soul. Later polls are far more favorable. It's a complex relationship, parenting. We go from a protective stance where we might imagine killing someone who harmed our child, to one in which we might yell, "I'm gonna kill that kid!" When bosom-buddy girlfriends get together to talk, it can include misty tears of gushy love, or there may be deep, wrenching sobs of grief.

Oh, My Child

Oh, you have broken me, my son
Just like a rock that's crushed to gravel
But speak one "Hey, I love ya' mom!"
those pieces stop, reverse their travel.

Oh, daughter you have pierced my heart!
Speared it completely, through and through.
but just one "Hey mom, you're the best!"
and I'm restored, as good as new.

No greater power on earth exists
to wreck or build or dominate
the sense of worth a parent feels
than the children they have helped create.

I Heard You In My Laugh

I giggled this morning
and thought I heard you!
I know you're the mirror
of much that I do.

But I'm just not too sure
which of us lays the path
cause I don't think before
I'm like that when I laugh.

I have seen me displayed
in the way that you walk
and I hear my advice
coming out when you talk.

It's a handed down thing
or perhaps handed up
when as mothers we sip
from a wee daughter's cup.

It's a treasure to me
like a pearl on the beach
since you've gone far away
where my arms cannot reach.

Missing my daughters

I So Be Loving You

Your little tiny toes
Your little dainty nose
Dark eyes and dark curls too
I so be loving you!

Oh, baby mine, so sweet
A dream we dreamed, complete
You made our dreams come true ...
We so be loving you!

Progeny

Listen my children, oh, listen I pray
Draw close to my side now, and heed what I say.
In life you'll be tested to be who ye be
You must then stand fast dears, oh, listen to me.

The priest, he will tell you how much you must give
The government tells you how rich you can live
There's a place that is sacred, deep inside of you
And it's there in your heart you must fight to be true.

I've taught what I know and it did well enough
For your childhood, but dearies, adulthood is tough!
While you have all the basics in place from my quest
Know this, 'twas a fable! Moms don't always know best.

Now as I draw close to the end of my life
I wish to prepare you to stand in such strife
Heed your spirit, my darlings, and do what ye must
I free you from my strings, into your own trust.

Go now, find the fullness, of what your life means
Remember my words, dears, when grief in you keens
You must be well rooted for life's stormy blows
So tend your own garden that the crop you choose grows.

Be then your own priest, your own governor, king
For the popular path may not be the right thing
God speaks to you each through that heart in your breast
And 'tis up to your listening to know what is best.

Be still now my darlings, for my strength seems to wane
Write your own Psalm of goodness, hold it fast in your brain
So you then can review how your pathway you've trod
It will strengthen you marking each blessing from God.

I'm not a wise woman, not near what you need
But you have so blessed me, my progeny seed
I give you my love and my fondest regard
I'll be watching and cheering from Heaven's back yard.

(I'll be right under the clothesline no doubt,
for I poured loving prayers on you while doing your laundry.)

Gallop, Waddle, Croak

If you can't run, then gallop!
Can't pirouette? Waddle!
Can't carry a tune? Do a frog!
Just do your full best as your gifts will allow
Don't retreat, lose yourself in a fog.

Don't limit yourself by society's rules
Who's to judge your best song's but a croak?
Cause samo-samo can get mighty old!
History proves status quo is a joke!

Adhere to the concept of "Different Drum!"
March your march while you beat your own speed!
That's how new benchmarks are laid out and won
Waddle, gallop and croak ... you'll succeed!

Family Circles

Ah, yes indeed, I do remember
All the joy that filled my heart
As I washed and dried those layettes
Little knew, they won't depart.

Didn't know the little suckers.
Never want to go away,
That they want to use our assets
And they never want to pay.

Didn't dream how they would use us
Tho we never let them lack,
Borrow stuff without us knowing
Sneak the shirt right off your back!

Still I treasure every memory
Little babes to bounce and dandle
Noting how they used us poorly
Is just more than I can handle.

Only parents know such suffering
Cuts like knife right to the bone.
There's no comfort in our watching
Their comeuppance from their own.

For it's gonna surely happen
Some day they will have a kid,
And we'd never want our lovies
To be done like we been did.

In the wisdom of The Ancients
It was planned, as you must know,
That the curses come to find those
Who screwed up so long ago.

Childhood Distress

Big measles, little measles, chicken pox!
Ear ache, tooth ache,
call the docs!
Hot fevers, cold shivers, mumps that fall,
Whooping cough, vomit, grow too short or tall.

Mosquito bites, bee stings, bloody nose
Head lice, scabies, hand-me-down clothes
Fall down, broken tooth, scraping hands and knees
Mommy get a Band-Aid and kiss it please.

Tummy ache, constipate, the back-door trots
Head cold, chest cold, sneezy snots.
Tonsillitis, 'ppendicitis, surgery
Stitches hurt, daddy! Please stay with me!

Castor oil, paregoric, iodine,
Hold your nose and stand in line.
Charley horse, restless legs, falling out of bed,
Insomnia, nightmares, bonks on the head.

Vaccination needles, fall down the stairs
Bite your tongue, gum stuck in your hairs.
Can't make it to the bathroom, wet your drawers.
Fall off bikes, slam fingers in the doors.

Climb up a tree, get splinters in your butt
Miss the baseball, get hit in the gut.
Ugly red pimples, picking scabs that bleed
Broken arms, broken legs, poison ivy weed.

There's a perfect explanation,
why we lived instead of died
mom and dad who gave us cautions,
then tanned our naughty hide.

Cups of Love

I recall blessed sips
of cold water at night
my mother brought to me
when I woke in fright.

Returned her the favor
when my little hands grew
by bringing her cups
of her favorite brew.

I still feel the touch
of her hand as we shared
and the depth of her eyes
as our thank yous we stared.

To this day I am grateful
when I see Nescafe
which allowed me that pay-back
in a child's simple way.

We cared for each other
as is taught from above
not with water or coffee,
but with cups full of love.

Mother Nose

God grants variety of gifts
Just right to meet each need
And mothers get a special nose
For tending to their seed.

Ours knew when milk was going sour
Soon as the lid came off
While others didn't smell a thing
And drank it with a scoff.

A hidden speck of mold in food
Could not escape her best
What others would brush off and eat
Would fail her mamma test.

From attic level bedroom
She could smell a basement mouse.
What made us think we'd get away
With smoking in the house?

The cookies she'd forbidden
Baked up for a neighbor's death
We'd sneak one, then get busted
She could smell them on our breath.

"We talked, that's all!" we'd tell her
Coming home late from a date.
She smelled the pheromones and beer
Before we'd latched the gate.

"Oh, darn that nose!" we'd mutter
As we told our vague white lies.
We knew to look beyond her
She could smell them in our eyes!

Her nose, beyond believing!
And we guess God gave her double
The gift He gives all mothers
To keep their children out of trouble.

Family Planning

Children are a blessing from the Lord
I learned that back in Sunday School.
Son-one arrived and proved it,
Sweetly obedient, so tender hearted.
Such a little man!
And thrilled, we felt so blessed,
Let's play that game again!

Thus came our second son
Oh it was quite the trick.
And we learned blessings
aren't all smooth like we had thought ...
Some pack a punch, a kick!

But, they blessed us good, those little men!
We waited then a bit and watched them grow,
Such fun, such joy, in spite of son-two's naughty show,
We wondered how things might turn out
Should we produce another wondrous little man ...
So much for our family plan.

Thus came a daughter to our home,
our Girlie Ann.
Girls are quite different you may know,
They can be whiners, selfish little things,
I knew she likely wouldn't show with wings.

She picked up qualities from them
Those brothers there to guide her every day,
Their wit, their kindness, and that other stuff
And spun them out in her own girly way.

A match for tender hearted little number One,
But spiced it up with color from the other,
They gave me quite a run, they did, those three,
And I feel mighty blessed to be their mother.

The Pleasure of You

In wonder I gaze at this miracle born
Tiny fingers and toes of such delicate hue
Neck soft, warm and fragrant
Lips a sweet Cupid-bow
Oh babe, I am lost in the pleasure of you.

Watching ancestry crossing your face as you sleep
Lives tied by this visiting genetic pool
But you are unique
Yes, you're one of a kind
I'm in love little child with the pleasure of you.

Imagining My Children

I can imagine rosy futures
I can imagine your success
I can't imagine how you'll get there
When you won't get up and dress.

From the sofa there's no progress
From supine there's no reward.
Life's exciting, don't you see that?
How can it be, you're always bored?

She stirs! Great God, imagine!
Has my lecture brought forth tears?
She wipes her eyes to move her hair
And I see buds stuck in her ears.

"What's to eat?" Croaks from the sofa
Broken, teenage manhood tone.
"Hang on, it's mom. I'll be right back."
He clearly speaks into his phone.

So engrossed in gadget games
They miss the joy of making stuff
From string, a can, a cardboard box
They think my childhood days were rough!

Folks from my own generation
Brought this E-lectronic age
And I really can't imagine
What these will face in "parent stage."

Their job's imagining the future
For those I'll call my "Grands," instead
Perhaps by then they'll beam, like Scotty
From gadgets these dreamed up in bed.

So They Say

Oh, I'm gonna be a gramma
So they say, so they say.
And the babe will come on some
November day, November day.

Feel a stirring in my heart
A place to lay, a place to lay
A little child to love forever
Come and stay! Oh, come and stay!

Step-Mothering

My mother was a marvel!
Raised my four older step-siblings
Right along with her own four.
Why wouldn't children
orphaned of a mother,
be happy to join a family circle
completed with a loving mother?
She made it look so easy
I thought she invented
Ozzy and Harriet!
I was so young I didn't see
how well she hid the pain and
sorrowing of step-mothering.
All I saw was her love for all.
And I was too young to know
of their suffering; their anger
over what they had lost.
A mother cannot be replaced
so easily in wounded hearts.

But my mother was a marvel!
And because of her bountiful love,
I helped raise someone else's children. They're family.
No problem
We added them into our circle of three.
I had so much love to share
Mother did it, so could I!
She cried when I told her.
I thought it would be easy-peasy!

It wasn't.

We started with two
and it was good.
Then the others needed homes,
so they were added,
after much thought.

Now, devastated and desperate lives outnumbered us,
an I.E.D. going off
right in the middle of our family.

Our happy home became a bomb crater.
I died. At least I thought I would.
Mothering in a war zone
was not my finest hour.
I didn't know I couldn't do this.

About WAR ZONES ...
Eventually,
Mother Nature takes them back,
and greens them over.
With a little help from human-kind ...
some careful planting, feeding, watering ...

those ugly places can become
a uniquely beautiful flower garden.

This dead woman ... me,
(Never happened, just escapist thinking ...)
allowed life to return.
Mother's Love bloomed again ...
not as I knew it before ...
a delicate, lacy, fragile, gushy thing ...

But a rugged, deep rooted,
enduring and ferocious hunger.
I guess I just grew up.
Step-motherhood did that.

I noticed the strangest thing ...
Volunteer blossoms of a hardy sort
Sprouting here and there
in the once scarred walls of my crater.
New life from things I planted long ago ...
I had watched them wither ...
I thought they died.

Now, in the greening, I see it,
the makings of a beautiful garden
... one of these days.

Mother Love and Laundry

When my daughter came to visit
Just before she went away
I took her basket to the laundry
And I slipped back in yesterday.

While smoothing out the wrinkles
folding everything just so,
Emotion flooded; loving feelings
A replay from some long ago.

Memories of hours of laundry
Ten to twenty loads a week
Sorting, soaking, mending, folding ...
Tears welled up; I couldn't speak.

While my fingers worked their magic
for my busy brood of seven
I was pouring love onto them
Whispering their names to heaven.

It was chilly in the laundry
But I really didn't know
Wrapped in gift from God, love's memories
Warming me, from head to toe.

Trauma Mamma

I couldn't handle happy times
as if I had no right!
But I responded in despair
and fought throughout the night.

The walking wounded face I wore
most surely signaled dread
And those I mothered
had to fear
that they soon would be dead.

Far from the truth, my darlings!
For I dead sure loved you so!
But I was much too childish then
a wiser way to go.

The little pond we swam in
as a family on the grow
was barely suited for the five
before you came, you know?

We all had lots of sorrows
That we drained into that pool
so swimming there was risky
when your life guard was a fool.

Oh, I was much too simple then
a homesick, lonely girl
who thought on
entering motherhood
that the skills would just unfurl.

Two sure regrets in raising you
was failure to rejoice
and knowing how to
help you grow
employing happier voice.

Humpty Dumpty

Cracked ... broken
Crushed ... scattered.
I have thrown myself
against your brick wall
of self-protection
until I'm splintered!

I don't need
all the kings horses
and all the kings men.
I just need one
to drag my sorry ass away
from this senseless and pointless game.
God forgive me for being so inadequate
that I can't reach into the heart of my own child!

Regret

I'm taking a swim
in the sea of regret
Tossed by memories of things
That I tried to forget.

Oh, If only you'd.
Or if only I'd
done it differently
Lord knows I have tried
to forget!
But here comes regret.

Your prison of stone
May have kept you
closed in
But we all served your time
and to your chagrin

Now your sentence is through
nothing here left of you
But to try and forget
and let go of regret.

Sweet Surrender

Ah, sweet surrender
How easy it is to do just that,
when life is sweet and love is in the air.
But here, now, is when we experience
surrender as sacrifice.

Picky, tricky, tightrope act
What do I owe, is this too much?
(Like prunes for constipated babies,
"Is one enough? Is two too many?")
And how much of me must be poured out?
Will there be any left of me to seek my bliss?
These are not babies, but adults who won't listen
to the wisdom of the elders all around them.
Won't stop their headstrong course
to think their actions through.

Here is sacred living:
I love me and them in the midst
of the stream turned to flood.
I pick my way to shore, and if I can save them
without drowning me, I will do so.
I am not a messiah nor a lamb.
I do not owe my life to any other this time 'round.
I have been sacrificed too many times before.

Safe, I will stand on the shore
and shout encouragement; throw a rope.
I will not go back down into the flood.
They must kick and swim and grab the rope.

Out, I will dry them, warm them
with a cup of tea and bid them peace.
It may be one of those times I am called to love,
and watch as they give up and go under.
And I will accept the outcome
of their making their own choices
without feeling guilty or responsible.
God is in heaven, all is well with the world.
I'm experienced at handling grief.
But I'm expert at new beginnings.
I'll be waiting.

Patch Work

Oh, I'm made of many a scrap
and I've been a many a thing
like a patch-work quilt I am
piecemeal, tied up fast with string.

With a remnant, dib, and dab
little samples from my past
from the pieces that remain
full blown memories shall last.
Oh, the wonderful colors!

MIRROR, Mirror, mirror

I'd come to know, accept myself
At last, down through the years.
So grateful God
has helped me shed
Bad habits, crippling fears.

And then there came
to live with me
Female descendants, three
My child, her child and
her child too
All bearing parts of me!

They all break out in silly song
All have artistic flair
All three have loving,
giving hearts
With empathy they share.

But I remember Mummy's curse
When I was in some stew,
"Oh little girl, I hope some day
You have a child like you!"

Those lesser qualities I owned
Got passed on, like the best.
It's noon,
and not one of the three
Has gotten themselves dressed!

Look at this mess, I fuss at them
For everywhere they touch
They leave some clutter
in their trail
Why be like me so much?

And sure as heck, like turtles,
They just suck themselves
right in
And I must wait
while they calm down
To nag them once again.

I wonder now if gramma may
Have said the same to her?
And noted similarities
That mother did confer?

Ah MIRROR, Mirror, mirror
Showing me reality
We pass our nature on like fruit
Right down our family tree.

Over Coffee

Came the day,
the babies came and we rejoiced,
Sharing and comparing
our darlings.
We slept when they slept.
There was never enough sleep.

Came the day,
they held our fingers
and walked on our feet
Then toddled on their own
and we were glad

Came the day
when being walked on
hurt a good deal,
and we cried in our sleep,
… if we slept.

Now comes the day,
we stand and move ourselves
from beneath a burden
too heavy for our own comfort.

Let's fluff out the places
that have been trampled
We'll sit where sun and soft
breezes can restore us!
My friend, I do so appreciate
your presence and support
through the joyful times,
and now
we struggle to shake off the grief
of lost dreams
and broken expectations.
My soul longs
for the peace we knew
when we sat
with our coffee,
Watching …
Watching personalities unfold,
dreaming of what might be.

In our journey together,
we promised to keep
our hearts open
To whatever changes may come.
Hang on, let's get walking
Perhaps,
there'll be sweet and calm sleep.

My love of poetry and penchant for writing came from my mother. She read a great variety of works to us and made sure we had books filled with her favorites. And she wrote. She wrote little poems on the brown paper bags we carried our lunches to school in, drawing cartoons to accompany them. She wrote poetic commentary on papers we left lying around; pithy retorts on the margins in books to show her displeasure with authors she thought didn't do their job well, or loving kudos to those who did. And she wrote a host of poems about what ever struck her fancy.

Most of all, she loved. She saw beyond the mundane, because of her enduring faith in God. She marked her children with her love and prayers and even traded us off to dear friends to pray for us while she prayed for their child when their frustration mounted. This is one of her poems:

Are All The Children In?

I think ofttimes as the night draws nigh
Of an old house on the hill.
Of a yard all wide and blossom starred
Where the children played at will.
And when the night at last came down
Hushing the merry din,
Mother would look around and ask,
"Are all the children in?"

'Tis many and many a year since then
And the old house on the hill
No longer echoes to childish feet
And the yard is still, so still.
But I see it all as the shadows creep
And though many the years have been
Even now it seems I can hear her ask
"Are all the children in?"

I wonder if, when the shadows fall
On the last short earthly day
When we say goodbye to the world outside
All tired with our childish play.
When we step out into the other land
Where mother so long has been
Will we hear her ask, as we did of old
"Are all the children in?"

© by Lucille Griffin O'Dell

GIRLS TALK ABOUT GRIEF and DEATH

I should not be surprised at how stoic people can be. Perhaps it's some lingering sense of duty to put others first, as we're taught in church. I learned well, in years of a nursing career, to shut off my own issues when interacting with my patients. Meanwhile I encouraged them to do something symbolic to commemorate their gains and losses.

Our culture can accept certain symbolic acts, but does not deal well with extreme shows of emotion. Personally, I tend to be rather dramatic. The opposite pole of my stoicism is the picture of a grief stricken woman sitting on the ground, tossing dust over herself and wailing out loud. It can be very expunging to "do" the pictures in one's head. Often, someone catches us at this game and wants to "fix" us. God bless'em.

Quandary: We can stifle ourselves to spare others their discomfort, distress and judgment, or we can act out our urges and bear the sidelong glances that tell us folks think we might be losing it, not just doing a play-acting-out. Enough research has been done on the mind/body/spirit connection to convince me of the value of acting out our visions in pursuing our healing; repressing emotions prolongs the suffering and may even lead to physical health issues. So I write my dramas.

Death, You Old Rascal

I've watched you,
down through the years ...
I struggled to pour life into veins
faster than you could empty them ...
You sat in the corner, stropping your razor ...
Ready to slice the life line, the silver cord ...
If I would just for one second, stop to wipe my brow.

I've glimpsed you lurking in cornfields
while broken bodies quiver and gasp for air in the ditch
and all that stands between you and the injured
is a silvery flicker, the glimmer of a hovering angel wing.

I saw you come down and out the birth canal,
the baby wrapped in your cloak, a waxen dolly
given and taken back before he saw the light of day
The young mother grasping to hang on,
and then following you into the forever together land.

We beat the air in vain, hanging IV bottles,
sucking up medications to shoot into the tubing
that led to hearts which beat no more.
Sometimes we won. Sometimes you stole our prize.

So I knew who I was dealing with
when my own beloved walked too near your trail.
I was informed and I was vigilant.
I was attentive. I was assertive ...
and then I stomped and screamed and raised hell!

It was as if they couldn't see you,
this team of strangers,
and there you were ... stropping to beat the band.

Did I stop to wipe my brow for just one second too long?
Did I give up too soon? Or had you just learned new ways
to sneak around me and attack where I wasn't watching?
You took me by surprise ... right in the middle of the sentence
my heart's love was speaking.
Cutting him off between "right" and "now."

Oh, you are soooo fast with that razor ...
I didn't even see the glitter ...
but I knew you had come and gone
quick as a flash ...
and you took my love with you.

You wily old bastard!

The Language Of Grief

It's a shrug of the shoulder
A shake of the head
What else can you say
When your loved one is dead

What words can describe
The great hole in your heart
With a fallout so massive ...
Just where do you start?

At the funeral parlor
It's easy to tell
Which ones of your callers
Have been through this hell.

By the shrug of a shoulder
The shake of a head
By their silent compassion
For no lies have they said

Like "It's gonna' get better"
Or "Your pain will soon fade."
Cause they know it's not true
Since their own pain has stayed.

If the language had words
It would fill up a book
Of enormous proportions
So we just use the look.

It shows up in the eyes
And great volumes are read
In the shrug of a shoulder
The shake of a head.

Sometimes

Count me among the saddened lot
who've lost a love or two,
(Sometimes their bodies just wear out
before their spirits do.)

Those left behind are slowly drained
by losses that cut deep.
We numbly fake our way through days
since our loved one went sleep.

I took some hits deep in my soul
and learned one thing that's true;
Sometimes our spirits just wear out
Before our bodies do.

I rage against this fate of mine,
No sweetness in my frame.
My heart cries out its litany
Each beat repeats your name.

I sense my soul in slippage
from the will to linger here.
I try to hide it from my friends
With a plastered face of cheer.

How long can I keep going
with a heart that's black and blue?
When my body, mind and spirit
Only want to be with you.

Sometimes we have to live by faith
And trust God has a plan
We'll be filled in on details when
we join with heaven's clan.

D-Day

They call this day, the 6th of June,
D-Day, the world around.
And we remember men who died
So freedom could abound.

But those around me know a name
Connected with this day
That name is Adam, Golden Boy,
Who loved and slipped away.

Desertion Day, Despairing Day
A day with sorrow fraught.
Depleted Day, Defeated Day
... We lost that war we fought.

This boy, young man, who did no war
But taught us bravery
Remains within our D-Day thoughts
In the land that's sweetly free.

Comparison

Our beautiful boy, so young you left
And all the world around us cared.
Our beautiful girl, still here, quite mad
And all around, no mercy spared.

Why is it thus, we dread the death
Of bodies taken from us?
But those who walk in deadened flesh
Provoke complaint and angry fuss?

Ensnared by physicality
Enslaved by wild mentality
Which the most dreaded fate to be?
I'll vote for death, with sanity.

Ah, God! Such thoughts!
I'd spare myself a lesson such as these,
but I've had both these horrid scenes
and pressed to choose the best for me …
Let me die, mentally intact.
Presuming I am.

He lived, knew love, gave love,
But she lives with a darkness
I can't see; responds with fear
It's fight and flee, from contact
with sweet folks like me.

Grief. Raw, when he left,
a dull ache now. Ah, God,
I tell you straight somehow,
we made it through that ghastly time,
Our lives go on, blond boys a chime
that ring the memories to life …
And her, oh, God, a constant strife.

Please give me hands that through her veil
can pierce, bring light, let love prevail …
Rescue her from her living hell …
I want to hear her sing your praises.

This grief, I need to let it go.
And trust, he came to tell me so …
Oh, Grammy, trust for her, like me,
for God is in control you see.
Well, you do not see, I know that clear,
His plan for her is held close, dear,
So dear, dear Grammy, please
let not your heart see trouble.
See her in health, your praises double.

Grief Works

I am sturdy, I'm no quitter
Great survivor, so they say
Here I stand to do my grief work
Pray that comfort comes my way.

Careful study; all the stages
Plan and do appropriate things
Show up for the grief support group
Why, you'd think I've sprouted wings!

That's the way I do my grief work,
Scientific as can be
... but no science in the mixing
when the grief is working me.

Grief works me in full-blown daytime
memories playing in my head
and it works me in the night time
tossing, turning in my bed.

Losing car keys, losing papers
losing time and losing track
Fail to eat and miss appointments
... tiny triggers brings grief back.

Neither rules nor bounds respected
by this adversary grim
but I've learned to bow and curtsey
grant attention due to him.

Once, I froze such fierce emotions
saving for some future days
till I found I'd formed a glacier
where no joy of living plays.

Now ... much older, somewhat wiser
I know not to run and hide
for what doesn't kill me outright
might just strengthen me inside.

Now when tears of grief are burning
I won't make them stay within
Let them empty like a river
Wash the grief outside my skin.

And when zingers stir my memories
Music, candles, coffee scent
I will celebrate our living
What our time together meant.

Belly Full of Grief

I do that
carry hard to bear things
deep in my belly.
Once, I had a belly full of anger
but after my great and soulful
loving affair
There was just no place
for anger.
Still, something was lurking
and I couldn't face it
any more readily
than I once faced the anger.

I walked in the cemetery,
searching for answers
fighting back the nausea
and then I did it
I let it have it's way with me.

Oh, I knew what it was, barely
I thought it was simply
grief, loss, sorrow

but it was more than that
the loss of my love
was the loss of half of me
and I can scarcely fathom
how my identity has diminished.

When I faced this grievous belly
and let it have its say
I retched and retched
emptying the woe
of un-cried tears and gall
into the grass
on a stranger's grave.

Drama, drama, drama!
Of such is my life
and of such is my healing.

Beginning to feel
A belly full of joy
for having known such love.

This Place of Shadows

In the shadow times,
Darkness thinks he is in charge
but he is not.
Light is the ruler.
Light is where we longingly
fix our gaze.

Meanwhile, Shadow presses
in for the kill, so he thinks,
urging Woe to run amok,
and with this unrelenting
behavior, leaping
and heaping on us,
and with his overplayed hand,
inadvertently creates
a playing field for the real boss.

For as shadows accumulate,
they coalesce into a puddle,
darkening everything
hiding ugly details
of ruined dreams
defeated hopes
into a soul stirring,
anonymous discontent.

How much easier then, to find
the merest pin-prick of light
from places lit by hope
by love ... grabbing the eye.

Those places
become a shining guide
and warriors lift their voices,
damning the darkness.
Enough of this!
And throwing open doors
allow Light enough
to lay the path
to leave Gloom behind.

Stay Close to Your Tree!

Just one of thousands leaflets,
that the lilac has on board.
Intoxicating vision, scent,
the glory of the Lord.

Life … life in fabulous array
the creatures who stop by
we dominate the springtime
and we hear the people sigh.

How wonderful the colors!
Oh, how sweet
the blossoms waft!
But leaves provide
a cooling shade
Till breeze brings winter's draft.

Soon scent and blossoms
fade away
No teeming life is found
Our color deepens ere we fall
to lie upon the ground.

Through autumn rain
and winter snow
Our numbers growing thin
Until remains, but one lone leaf
Upon a barren limb.

A gift indeed, to those who sighed
and watched our springtime show
But I alone, am witness to
Their joy that I won't go.

A service I have given them,
a lesson they can take,
That flash and flair are wondrous
But do not a warrior make.

For it's about connection here
fast clinging to my tree
When all about seems lost
and bleak
That lends such strength to me.

Soon I will join my brothers there
Where I still serve the tree
Perhaps to make a blossom next
When springtime calls for me.

Time Out of Control

Time rolls me
by hour and by date
like a snowball
head over heels
down the steep slopes of life.

Only the fear of a calamitous end
against some obstacle ...
A tree ... a boulder ...
Another loss of love
Leading to a long drop into the abyss
causes me to struggle to free myself
stop this hypnotic plunge
and regain control
of my calendar,
my clock,
my mind.

Whatever Happened to Hansel and Gretel?

I don't know how to go on with life.
I just follow the breadcrumbs of inspiration
that show up in my brain.
Have to jump on them quick
before the hungry birds of sorrow come to feed.

JELLOeMotions

If feelings could be stirred up
like a gelatin dessert ...
I'd do up some emotions
in a way that cannot hurt.

My anger would be cherry red
and molded like a star.
With sharpened tips to point out
when I think you've gone too far.

My sadness would be cobalt blue
a sphere, no end, no start
Or maybe add a pointy end
And shape it like a heart.

If I feel down, crushed like a grape
I'd cut this one in squares
And stand upon my own soapbox
to kick aside those cares.

My envy would be limey green
and mashed into a slurry
I'd give this one no substance
for it kills joy in a hurry.

My happiness is lemon bright
and molded like the sun
Considering all these choices
this could be my favorite one!

Long Arm of the Law

I reach my hand to take the phone
the distance telescopes away
so I content myself and think
I'll call some folks another day.

I touch the keypad, try to dial
and find the digits can't be pressed
Intentions meet a glassy wall
I hang in air and feel depressed.

My fingers wander on the keys
No words will form within my brain.
Though my intentions are so good
Inertia Laws have won again.

I haven't written, haven't called
My projects lay upon the shelf.
Some day this grieving must resolve
and I'll get back to my old self.

No Tears

You'll see no tear track
on my cheek
Nor welling in my eye
But you may hear a
pounding rain
If I forget and sigh.

I walk this path, unsought by me
To carve a brand new start.
Ignoring torrents made of tears
That would erode my heart.

The Blue Gone Dream

Oh my love, my love!
Didn't you hear me calling,
"Don't go! Come back!"
But even as I called, you were gone.

Before you were gone ...
GONE
was a word for empty wine bottles
for discarded peanut butter jars
used up jam pots and empty bread wrappers
It was a word for the mound of cellophane twists
overflowing the candy dish beside your chair
A word for exhausted paper cores
left on the holder in the bathroom
when you left there with a smile.
There has never been a gone
so very gone
as your absence has created.

You are gone from here
but never from my heart and soul.
I see you watching in my blue gone dreams.

From the Other Side, They Comfort Us

Looks different from the other side ...
We run from death, but we can't hide.
The angels show up, mild and sweet
Take some away, the Lord to meet ...

By lot, appointment, or design
Rejoice or weep, those left behind
Bereft, to think that we don't care
and gladly flew to leave them there ...

Here from the Vault of Heaven, I
can see their pain and gently sigh.
I try to give them comfort now
and send a breeze to cool a brow.

Or ring the wind chimes by the door
which we enjoyed so much before.
Or stamp my symbols in the sky
In cloudy pictures floating by.

Or show my face deep in the night
when clouds are lit with silvery light
I touch his shoulder, smooth her hair
Send dreamtime eagle, crow or bear.

And maybe once, leave heaven's bliss
and journey back to plant a kiss
on lips that long for mine to come ...
... but heaven now's my favored home.

Time Blinks

A blink in time
from start to end
our lives play out
and they are done.

In God's time line
I know that we
will reunite
by morning's sun.

But here beneath
heaven's canopy
Time runs another
dance and song

And blinks add up
to billions here
Till we unite, love,
much too long.

I hear that to find pristine, wild land in North America we must now go to western Canada. So much of our own is under millions of pounds of concrete and steel or is unusable because we have poisoned it. Now they say the oceans have been disastrously over fished and heavily polluted. Mountains are leveled for the coal or ore inside them, spilling the dross into the valleys, clogging streams and destroying habitat of wild and tamed things. There are those who rejoice each time a gigantic new machine chews its way through the breast of Mother Earth and claims some new area, as if wilderness is an enemy. There are many who do not rejoice, and we weep with her.

Weep, Oh Earth!

Weep, oh, Earth!
Thy lot's been drawn
to incubate
mankind's birth dawn.

And weep ere more
'tis told that he
shall propagate
to conquer thee!

His arrogance
will take your breath
Oh, pray for aide
that stays your death!

Water and air
and all the land
Weep now in dread
of mankind's hand!

Crossing the Pond

I've decided
not to live my life hopping from grief to grief
on a hundred little anniversaries of loss

Like a frog crossing the pond
jumping from lily pad to lily pad,
above still and dark waters
Unable to see where I'm headed
on such a fragile and lowly perch
Never reaching solid footing.

Instead ...
I will take purposeful strides
across the flowing river of life
Stepping from stone to stone ...
There, high above the water
I can choose a course
Calling on the wisdom,
courage and strength
of those who came my way
and now are gone.

Each successful step
A reminder of the blessings
each brought into my life ...
And I will thank God
that loss can become gain.

Walking In the Sun

I've decided not to live my life
Playing "Ain't it Awful?"
Every time some sorrowful thing
Crosses my sky,
Or skies of those I love,
Blotting out the sunshine for a spell.

Neither will I indulge
In self-flagellation
Playing, "Ain't I Awful?"
As if I control the skies!

I walked The Gracious Pathway, trusting God,
and I grew.
I will not deny another their own lessons
By trying to "fix" their path.
I share my umbrella,
And I walk in the sun
In spite of the rain.

(My intention is
To live my beliefs.
To love
To look at the most positive possible view
of what occurs.
To praise The Living God)

Gayle, Ghandi and The Godfather
all decided to grow tomatoes
upon retirement from controlling.

ABOUT THE POET

"Every thing, and every thought, can be turned into a poem, much like all food can be turned into soup," Bobbie Gayle Dailey says. She does just that, drawing from her experiences raising a mixed family of seven, various pets, and a hospital nursing career spanning forty-two years. She worked in surgery, emergency, medical, surgical, cardiac, psychiatry, labor and delivery, and management roles. She also took clients privately as a Rebirthing-Breathworker. "I loved the sense of sacredness in caring for people. I felt honored to be present at birth, death and the emotional thin-ice times in between."

Bobbie was born at home, the next to youngest in an extended family in a thriving coal mining community in West Virginia. Her mother, also a poet, instilled a love of humor, music, reading, and a strong spiritual interest. Now a retired R.N. living in Southern Oregon, Bobbie enjoys gardening, fishing, water coloring, camping, family and friends. A regular participant at The Second Friday Poetry Sharing at The Grants Pass Museum of Art, she is also a five year Blue Ribbon winner at the county fair in the poetry category.

Interested in holistic approaches, she considers her subject matter from body, mind, and spirit, often finding the drama and spiritual implication in mundane things. "Until I seriously started writing, I was ashamed of my dramatic flair. I know my style is gritty at times, but I try not to be shocking. There is no such thing as TMI for a nurse. This is life!" she declares.

Made in the USA
San Bernardino, CA
04 May 2017